Favorite CLASSICAL Melodies

FLUTE

Arranged and Recorded by David Pearl
("Brandenburg Concerto No. 5, First Movement" arranged and recorded by Donald Sosin)

Cherry Lane Music Company
Director of Publications/Project Supervisor: Mark Phillips

ISBN: 978-1-60378-402-3

Visit our website at www.cherrylaneprint.com

CONTENTS

AVE MARIA

FLUTE

By Charles Gounod and Johann Sebastian Bach

BRANDENBURG CONCERTO NO. 5, FIRST MOVEMENT

By Johann Sebastian Bach

FLUTE

5

CARO MIO BEN

FLUTE

By Giuseppe Giordani

CLAIR DE LUNE

FLUTE

By Claude Debussy

FUNERAL MARCH OF A MARIONETTE

FLUTE

by Charles Gounod

Moderately fast, in 2

GYMNOPÉDIE NO. 1

FLUTE

By Erik Satie

HALLELUJAH CHORUS

from *Messiah*

By George Frideric Handel

FLUTE

Moderately fast

HUNGARIAN DANCE NO. 5

FLUTE

By Johannes Brahms

MINUET
(from String Quintet in E Major)

By Luigi Boccherini

FLUTE

PIANO SONATA NO. 14 "MOONLIGHT"

First Movement

By Ludwig van Beethoven

FLUTE

SYMPHONY NO. 5
First Movement

FLUTE

By Ludwig van Beethoven

WILLIAM TELL OVERTURE

FLUTE

By Gioacchino Rossini

POMP AND CIRCUMSTANCE

FLUTE

By Edward Elgar